Christmas Treasures of the Heart

by
Cheri Fuller

Tulsa, Oklahoma

Christmas Treasures of the Heart
ISBN 1-56292-182-7
Copyright © 1996 by Cheri Fuller
P. O. Box 770493
Oklahoma City, Oklahoma 73177

Published by Honor Books, Inc.
P. O. Box 55388
Tulsa, Oklahoma 74155

A Note to Lovers of Christmas

"And all the loveliest things there be;
come simply, or so it seems to me."
Edna St. Vincent Millay.

Many of the loveliest things about the Christmas season are simple: making cookies, smelling the fragrance of a fresh evergreen wreath, or receiving a card from a long-lost friend. This book celebrates those simple joys with poems, quotes, creative ideas, stories, and customs. Making warm memories and enjoying traditions is part of the holiday season, and whether it's reading the Nativity story on Christmas Eve, caroling in your neighborhood, or decorating the tree with handmade ornaments, traditions are treasures of the heart, enjoyed in the present and cherished through the years.

Christmas Treasures of the Heart is full of ideas and inspiration for celebrating Christmas without the pressure of creating the "perfect Christmas" or doing everything right. We can find the real meaning of the season by simple hospitality, generosity, and spending time with those who need it most — causing some of the most precious experiences at Christmastime.

Toy trains and electronic gadgets get broken and even the finest gifts may wind up in a garage sale, but the tapestry of memories woven from family traditions, helping others, being with friends, and holiday fun last a lifetime. Enjoy this book, and if an idea strikes you as something your family would enjoy, use it now or save it for next year. Most of all, have a Merry Christmas!

Create a Quilt of Memories

to keep me warm.

An inner warmth that comes from happy times.

Weave in the threads of holidays, of friends and families...

Delights of seashore, fields, of city parks.

The simplest happenings traced out in love

become a pattern, for my quilt of memories.

— Ruth Reardon

Christmas Is Coming!

- Get out holiday dishes
- Play Christmas music
- Make and hang a family wreath

- Have a candlelight meal: Light a group of candles in the center of table. Use your best china. Turn out the lights. Whether you serve a Holiday Fiesta or another dish, it will seem more special by candlelight. Have each person share something he is grateful for in the past year.

Christmas...the season of gifts great and small when joy is the nicest gift of all.

Holiday Fiesta

$\mathcal{B}$rown ground beef and drain. Arrange in colorful bowls: chopped tomatoes, chopped black olives, onions, picante sauce, guacamole, pinto and kidney beans. In a large bowl put lots of chopped lettuce, and fill a sombrero with tortilla chips. Provide warm flour and corn tortillas, rice and refried beans. Let each person make his own fiesta salad and burritos.

Hang a pinata, play Spanish music, and read a Christmas story from Mexico to enjoy a "South of the Border" evening. Serve pralines for dessert and enjoy!

Make A Family Welcome Wreath

*T*ake a green wreath and decorate it with whatever characterizes the special memories and interests of each family member during the past year: a trip memento, a tiny bride & groom to remember a family wedding, a small ballet shoe, etc. With florist wire and picks, attach these items to wreath. Weave bright thin ribbon in and out. Hang the wreath on your front door to welcome all who come through during the holiday season. After Christmas, cover wreath with plastic and save the memories of your year.

8

Christmas Wreath

Symbolizing eternal hope,

the wreath goes 'round and 'round,

And where it starts or ends cannot be found.

Woven of things that grow — for life,

and hung for holiday delight

The wreath must be left in place

From Advent through Twelfth Night.

— Anonymous

9

There are two ways to live your life.

One is as though nothing is a miracle.

The other is as though everything is a miracle.

— Albert Einstein

Let us remember that the Christmas heart is a giving heart, a wide-open heart that thinks of others first. The birth of the baby Jesus stands as the most significant event in all history, because it has meant the pouring into a sick world of the healing medicine of love which has transformed all manner of hearts for almost two thousand years...Underneath all the bulging bundles is this beating Christmas heart.

— George Matthew Adams[1]

11

The Gifts Most Dear

Of all the gifts

I have each year,

some sparkling,

bright and glowing,

I think the gifts

I hold most dear

Are ones so green and growing.

— Anonymous

Christmas Bulbs

*N*othing makes a more cheerful decoration or thoughtful (and inexpensive) gift as a pot of bulbs that bloom in winter.

- Choose an interesting container: a pottery dish or basket or bowl.

- Set Paper White Narcissus bulbs or Red Amaryllis bulbs in container, at least 3" deep, filled with pebbles or gravel.

- Keep in cool, dark place for 2 weeks and then move to a bright spot.

- Encircle container with a bright red ribbon and give something green and growing!

Do not think that love,

in order to be genuine,

has to be extraordinary.

What we need is to love

without getting tired...

Be faithful in small things

because it is in them

that your strength lies.

— Mother Teresa

Give the gift of kind words today!

Encouraging words can change someone's whole perspective and
work a miracle:

>Loving words will cost but little,
>Journeying up the hill of life;
>But they make the weak and weary
>Stronger, braver, for the strife.
>
>Do you count them only trifles?
>What to earth are sun and rain?
>Never was a kind word wasted;
>Never was one said in vain.

— Anonymous

15

A Gift of Love from the Heart...

Think of your spouse, child, or friend's favorite interest, hobby, or passion. Give something today that would enhance that interest: a sketch pad for someone who likes to draw and paint, flower seeds and a trowel for the gardener, a biography of a great person in history for the history buff, a basket of small notes for one who loves to write letters.

Child's Play!

When kids have an opportunity to make presents, they love to be creative! I remember the fun my sisters and I had making a holiday tablecloth for Mother's dining table out of red net, felt, and sequins. Pick a Saturday or evening and gather some children to find "joy in the making."

> May the child who lives with us
> Gently teach us how to find
> Joy and trust in one another —
> Lasting faith in all mankind.
>
> — Anonymous

Gift to Make:
Glitter Christmas Balls

- Pour glitter into a bowl

- Brush white glue on a Styrofoam ball wherever you want to apply glitter

- Dip ball into the bowl

- Hang or prop the ball to dry

- Brush off excess glitter

- Glue thin (1/4") silver or gold ribbon around top

Gift to Make:
Gourmet Bean Soup Mix

*I*n a zip-lock bag put: 1/2 cup each of split green peas, lentils, baby limas, black turtle beans, and pinto beans.

Write the recipe on a card: In an 8-quart Dutch oven, combine beans with 2 T. chopped parsley, 1 bay leaf, 3/4 t. thyme & marjoram. Add 10 c. chicken stock. Bring to a boil, and skim off foam. Reduce heat and simmer 2 1/2 hours until beans are tender. In skillet, sauté 1 chopped onion, 4 chopped carrots, 3 celery ribs and 2 cloves minced garlic in a little oil. Stir into beans and stock. Add 1/2 lb. cubed ham, 1 large can diced tomatoes, 1 T. mustard, salt & pepper. Simmer and enjoy! Decorate card and staple as label.

What Makes a Happy Family?

In a nationwide survey, thousands of school children were asked what they thought makes a happy family. The kids didn't answer a big house, designer jeans, or CD players. The most-mentioned key to happiness was "DOING THINGS TOGETHER."

Kids' Cooking Party

*H*ere's a great way to show hospitality to your kids and their friends, your grandchildren, or the neighborhood children when school lets out for the holidays. Before your young friends arrive, make or buy large gingerbread people cookies and provide raisins, colored icing (or small store-bought tubes of red and green frosting), red hots, sprinkles, or other candy decorations.

You'll find that the kids will love creating their own fantasy people and making their own gingerbread family to take home!

"You're here to bring light, bringing out all the God colors in the world...If I make you light-bearers, you don't think I'm going to hide you under a bucket, do you? I'm putting you on a light stand. Now that I've put you on a hilltop, on a light stand — SHINE!"

— Matthew 5:14-16, *The Message*

We light candles to symbolize the glorious bright light upon the stable that first Christmas night in Bethlehem, when Christ's life and light entered our dark world. Here are some ways to "light up" the lives of all who enter your home:

- Give someone a little basket full of small votive scented candles.

- Get a little string of tiny white twinkle lights and tack around your child's bedroom window.

- On Christmas Eve, turn down the lights, have each family member hold a lighted candle, share a holiday memory, and sing "Silent Night."

The means to gain happiness

is to throw out from oneself,

like a spider,

in all directions

an adhesive web of love,

and to catch in it

all that comes.

— Leo Tolstoy

The Tinsel on the Tree

Long ago a good widow with many children to care for cut a Christmas tree in the nearby forest. Trying to survive on little income from baking for the townspeople, she had no money for decorations. She and her children made snowflakes from scraps of paper they had saved and trimmed it as beautifully as they could with the little they had. During the night as they slept, spiders visited the tree, crawling from branch to branch. As they left their shimmering webs behind, an angel came and transformed all the spider webs into shining silver.

A Child's Christmas Tree

It's wonderful for kids to have a smaller tree to decorate in any way they choose. Making their own ornaments also keeps them busy on days when it is too cold or rainy to play outside.

Put the little tree in a sturdy holder on a table. Beside it provide construction paper for making chains, glitter, glue, and other materials.

The children's tree can be as unique as their interests: a sports tree hung with baseball cards, a tree decorated with bright origami (Japanese paper-folding), or a tree covered with small paper airplanes colored with markers.

God grant you the light in Christmas which is faith;

the warmth of Christmas, which is love;

the radiance of Christmas, which is purity;

the righteousness of Christmas, which is justice;

the belief in Christmas, which is truth;

the all of Christmas, which is Christ.

— Wilda English

Joy to the World!

Joy to the world! the Lord is come;

Let earth receive her King;

Let ev'ry heart prepare Him room,

And heav'n and nature sing,

And heav'n and nature sing,

And heav'n, and heav'n and nature sing.

— Isaac Watts

I am not alone at all, I thought. *I was never alone at all*. And that, of course, is the message of Christmas. We are never alone. Not when the night is darkest, the wind coldest, the world seemingly most indifferent. For this is still the time God chooses.

— Taylor Caldwell[2]

A Joyful Single Christmas

I have discovered that being *alone* on Christmas Day does not have to be *lonely*. There are so many good people who are willing to share the day with others who are alone, and I usually always have an invitation to go somewhere. As a guest, though, I also realize that families enjoy being alone for at least part of the morning to open their presents, so I usually decline going until noon; hence, I have the morning to myself and they have their "family time" together.

So, I have devised a great diversion that has never failed to give me much joy and beauty on Christmas morning even though I am alone. After a special breakfast, devotions, and reading my Bible, I spend the rest of the time reading my Christmas cards, which I have saved for the entire month just for Christmas morning. I savor every note and the meaning on the cards themselves. Sometimes it takes me two hours or more to read all the cards, and I certainly can't be lonely with so many well wishes. There just is no sense worrying about what I don't have, when I really have so much! By that time, I am hurrying to get ready to go out for the day, in a cheerful mood and ready to entertain and be entertained on this blessed holiday.

— Beverly Rhoades

The Birds at Christmas

I heard a bird sing

In the dark of December

A magical thing

And sweet to remember.

— Oliver Herford

At Christmas, remembering our feathered friends is not only an enduring tradition, it's a good way to care for, "all creatures great and small." Here are some ways:

- Make a holiday bird treat by rolling pine cones in a peanut butter and honey mixture and then in bird seed. Tie on a thin wire to hang on a tree branch.

- String fresh cranberries and popcorn on thread and decorate an outdoor tree.

- Spray-paint some wooden birdhouses red or gold to hang from trees, and then fill them with sunflower seeds.

May thy Christmas

happy be,

And naught

but joy appear,

Is now the wish

I send to thee,

And all I love

most dear.

— Victorian Christmas Card verse

Day Before Christmas

We have been helping with the cake
And licking out the pan,
And wrapping up our packages
As neatly as we can.
And we have hung our stockings up
Beside the open grate,
And now there's nothing more to do
Except to wait!

— Marchette Chute

An informal survey of adults shows that what most people want for Christmas is two more weeks to prepare for it!

35

A friend sent Clement Moore's "A Visit From St. Nicholas" to a local newspaper. It was extremely well received, but Dr. Moore waited 16 years to admit to being the author of what became the beloved poem "The Night Before Christmas." As a professor of theology and literature, he was afraid the poem would damage his academic standing.

Santa is a dramatic emblem of a world crying out for
a larger-than-life daddy who will love his kids
even when they are not perfect
and give them gifts to fulfill their longings.

— Jack Hayford

Bright Idea!

Write a letter on decorative paper to each one of your children (or friends) noting their personal growth and changes during the year, what you're grateful for about them — the virtues, personality and character qualities you admire. Put it in an envelope and stick it in their stocking or tie the letter on a branch of the Christmas tree.

Let me be a little kinder, let me be a little blinder To the faults of those about me Let me praise a little more.

— Anonymous

It is Christmas every time you let God love others through you...yes, it is Christmas every time you smile at your brother and offer him your hand.

— Mother Teresa

Each Christmas we share
With friends both far and near
Makes our years together
So memorable and dear.

— Anonymous

39

Share the Spirit of Christmas Love:

- Offer to drive a homebound person to see the holiday decorations and lights around your city.

- Cook an extra casserole of a Christmas entrée and give it to a friend who's been ill.

- Contact a homeless shelter to see what they need most: blankets, gloves, etc. Then gather donations and deliver them before Christmas.

- Have each member of the family save a portion of what they are spending on gifts, pool it, and decide on a local charity to which you could donate it.

Classic Christmas Movie Night

Gather family or friends together with take-out pizza or Chinese food. Get quilts and sleeping bags to snuggle up in by the fire. Have on hand plenty of popcorn and cider. Watch a favorite old Christmas movie video and watch the stress of this busy season drain out of everyone.

Here are some nostalgic holiday videos you won't want to miss: "Meet Me in St. Louis," "A Christmas Carol," "It's a Wonderful Life," "Miracle on 34th Street," and modern ones, "The Santa Clause" and "A Muppet's Christmas Carol."

On one branch there hung little nets cut out of colored paper, and each net was filled with sugar plums, and among other boughs gilded apples and walnuts were suspended...little blue and white tapers were placed among the leaves.

— Clement C. Moore

Christmas-tide Comes in like a Bride

When Christmas-tide comes in like a bride,

With holly and ivy clad,

Twelve days in the year,

Much mirth and good cheer

In every household is had.

— from *The Praise of Christmas*, 1630

Christmas Across the Miles

One December we were 2,000 miles away from family. I wanted to get gifts for my young nieces and nephews, but money was very tight. So I searched at our local library for some of the best Christmas stories: a Russian tale called "Babushka," a book of Christmas legends, "The Gift of the Magi," and others. I checked out the books, bought blank tapes and decorated white folder labels with holly and the titles of the stories. Then I sat down by a glowing fire and read these stories aloud while making a cassette tape for each of my nieces and nephews. A few days later, I got a call from my sister. "Josh loved the Christmas story tape you sent!" she said. "He's listened to the stories over and over, and even took the tape recorder to bed with him and fell asleep while listening."

Although I couldn't be with my family that year, the warm feeling I got from making personal story tapes and hearing about their enjoyment made the time it took to read and prepare them worthwhile. You could record a tape with your child reading Christmas stories and then send it to a grandparent or a visually impaired person.

Welcome here, welcome here

All be alive and be of good cheer.

I made a loaf that's cooling there,

With my neighbors I will share.

come, all ye people,

hear me sing

A song of friendly welcoming...

— Traditional Shaker verse

Make-Ahead Christmas Cranberry-Orange Bread

Perfect to make and give to friends or serve at holiday meals, or make and freeze ahead.

2 cups sifted flour
1-1/2 t. baking powder
1/2 t. soda
1 cup sugar
1/2 t. salt

1 egg
1 cup raw, diced cranberries
1 cup pecans, chopped
1 orange

- Juice and grate rind of orange; add 2 T. oil and fill cup with boiling water
- Mix dry ingredients; add wet ingredients, cranberries, pecans. Bake in greased, floured pans for 45-50 min.

Baking Tips for Christmas Kitchens

- Buy sacks of fresh cranberries before Thanksgiving, when they are plentiful, and freeze them for holiday baking.

- Make up extra sugar cookie dough and freeze in frozen juice cans. Then push out, slice, decorate and bake!

- To fill your home with smells of Christmas, bake apples with lots of brown sugar, cinnamon and raisins — and serve them for dinner dessert!

- Fill a basket or crock with unshelled nuts, a nutcracker, and invite kids and family members to enjoy the nuts and chat while you cook.

Strawberry Bread

3 cups flour
2 cups sugar
1 t. baking soda
1 t. salt

2 10-oz. packages frozen
   strawberries, defrosted
4 eggs
1 cup oil

Mix all ingredients and add 1 cup chopped pecans if desired. Bake at 350 degrees for 50 minutes to 1 hour. Makes 2 loaves. For a delicious icing, mix 8 ounces cream cheese and juice from the strawberries until it's a frosting consistency. Wrap loaves in red cellophane and tie with a ribbon for a festive gift, or enjoy Christmas morning.

How grand and how bright

That wonderful night

When angels to Bethlehem came.

They burst forth like fires

They struck their gold lyres

And mingled their sound with the flame.

—17th Century English carol

The Joy of Giving

Somehow not only for Christmas
But all the long year through,
The joy that you give to others
Is the joy that comes back to you.
And the more you spend in blessing
the poor and lonely and sad,
The more of your heart's possessing
Returns to make you glad.

— John Greenleaf Whittier

Beat the Holiday Blues

Many people find themselves depressed around the Christmas season. If you do, here are some ways to lift your spirits:

- Regularly visit someone confined to a hospital bed or nursing home.

- Make something for a needy child (a wooden toy or knitted gloves, for example).

- Ring the Bell for Salvation Army.

- Get up early one morning, have a hot cup of cider, and watch the sun come up!

Keep the Ho-Ho-Ho in the Holiday

*I*nstead of entertaining wishful fantasies about keeping a perfect house while your children are home for the holiday, or having an ideal, storybook Christmas:

- Designate an hour when the whole family pitches in to clean and shine everything that's visible; save the deep-cleaning for a rainy January day.

- If you don't have time to do a Christmas letter, write it for Valentine's Day instead!

- Avoid getting so busy that you stop exercising. If you take a brisk walk or exercise daily, you'll have more energy and a cheerful attitude.

Sharing a Christmas Classic

Every night before bed in December, read a Christmas story to your child.

> Life holds no sweeter thing than this:
> To teach a little child the tale most loved on earth
> And watch the wonder deepen in his eyes
> There while you tell him of the Christ Child's birth;
> The while you tell him of shepherds and a song,
> Of gentle drowsy beast and fragrant hay
> On which that starlit night in Bethlehem
> God's tiny Son and His young mother lay...

> — Adelaide Love

Our house is open, Lord, to Thee;

Come in and share our Christmas tree!

We've made each nook and corner bright,

Burnished with yellow candlelight.

But light that never burns away

Is only thine, Lord Jesus, stay;

Shine on us now, our Christmas Cheer —

Fill with Thy flame our whole New Year!

— Luci Shaw

Christmas Hot Chocolate

"*N*o hot chocolate on Christmas Eve?" Christine asked.

"Next year," her mom Cheryl promised as she dressed for the midnight service.

Having hot chocolate on Christmas Eve was a family tradition, but this year they couldn't afford even that. Jack, the dad, had been laid off months earlier; their car was broken down; food was scarce, and the family's financial picture was growing bleaker each day.

> *No act of kindness*
> *No matter how small*
> *Is ever wasted.*
>
> — Aesop

Later, as they sat in the candlelight service, Cheryl prayed silently, "Oh, Lord, you promised to take care of us. Have you forgotten?"

Joyful songs and hope rang out as people filed out of the church, but Cheryl's heart was heavy. Just then, their daughter's youth director called to them: "Wait!" She pulled a brightly ribboned jar from her bag — hot chocolate mix! "Merry Christmas!" she said.

This kind friend didn't know of their family tradition, or that to Cheryl, this simple gift was a reminder that God had not forgotten their family after all.

The Gift Of Hospitality — A Holiday Dessert Party

*I*nvite your friends to an evening of warm fellowship and delicious desserts. Ask each person to bring her favorite dessert or cookies and a can of food for a Christmas basket for the needy. Serve a tray of fruit and cheese, a pot of flavored coffee, and hot cinnamon tea. Then top the evening off by telling stories by the fire.

> *The most essential thing for happiness is the gift of friendship.*
> — Sir Wm. Osler

Christmas Caroling Party

The weekend before Christmas, there's nothing more fun than inviting a few families (including children) and single friends to go out caroling together in the neighborhood, in a hospital ward, or a nursing home. After caroling, gather inside and warm the caroler's hands and hearts with steaming cups of apple cider and a light potluck supper, or a big pot of chili and a loaf of French bread.

Giving Gifts From the Heart

*A*lthough these gifts may not cost much, they will be cherished by the recipient:

- **Coupon Kindness**

  Give a family member or friend a coupon with a promised service: for a friend, a dessert you'll make the next time she has company for dinner; for your child — a day at the science museum with you. A gift from a child might read: "This coupon entitles you to breakfast in bed any Saturday of your choice in the month of January."

> *The poorest human being has something to give that the richest could not buy.*
>
> — George M. Adams

- **A Gift of Teaching**
  Share love at Christmas by helping someone learn your skill. One dad gave his teenage son lessons in computer programming. A mom I know gave her daughter sewing lessons. A musician I know gave her friend guitar lessons.

- **The Gift of Listening**
  Open your heart to someone over a cup of tea and hear their stories, hopes, and dreams.

It Came Upon A Midnight Clear

It came upon a midnight clear,
That glorious song of old,
From angels bending near the earth
To touch their harps of gold;
"Peace on the earth, good will to men,
From heav'n's all gracious King."
The world in solemn stillness lay
To hear the angels sing.

— Edmund Sears & Richard S. Willis

The time draws near

The birth of Christ

The moon is hid;

The night is still

The Christmas bells from hill to hill

Answer each other in the mist.

— Alfred, Lord Tennyson

A Christmas Web

A holiday activity that originated in the Victorian era, the Christmas Web is fun for all ages to play on Christmas Eve, during a family gathering, or children's holiday party.

Get a small gift and a ball of string or yarn (in different colors) for each member of the family or party. Fasten a different color string to each of the gifts. Hide the gifts in various places around the house, and then wind the string through the house, looping around furniture, through chair legs and stair banisters, over curtain rods, etc. — making a colorful and complicated web. All strings end at the doorway and are attached to strips of cardboard for rewinding. Hand each player his or her cardboard spool and watch the delight begin as the strings are rewound and the gifts are discovered. The winner is the first person to find his gift, untangle the string, and wind it into a ball.

Christmas Straw

*E*ncourage kindness and unselfishness in the family by starting the tradition of "Christmas Straw": First collect some straw and place it in a basket by the side of an empty little cradle or basket representing a manger. On the day you begin, draw names. Then during the days ahead, each person does a thoughtful deed each day without their recipient knowing it (like making his bed for him while he's in the shower or polishing her shoes while she's at work).

> *The best Christmas gift of all is the presence of a happy family all wrapped up with one another...in love.*

These little acts of kindness have nothing to do with money or "store-bought" gifts. Instead, they are ways of meeting the needs of others. They may include leaving a note of encouragement or making a treat.

Each time someone does a thoughtful deed, he gets to place a bit of straw in the manger. By Christmas Eve, Baby Jesus (a doll wrapped in a "swaddling blanket" or nativity character) has a cradle full of straw on which to lie.

Bring forth

the fir tree,

The box,

and the bay,

Deck out

our cottage

For glad

Christmas day!

— Anonymous Old English verse

Joy

Joy seems to me a step beyond happiness —

happiness is a sort of atmosphere

you can live in sometimes when you're lucky.

Joy is a light that fills you

with hope and faith and love.

— Adela Rogers St. Johns

One Starry Night

$\mathcal{F}$ive hundred years ago Martin Luther, German leader of the Protestant Reformation, began the custom of decorating Christmas trees.

While walking through the woods one beautiful starry night near Christmas Eve, Luther gazed at a large evergreen tree illuminated by the starlight. He was struck by the incredible sight, which reminded him of the night the angels appeared to the shepherds in Bethlehem, announcing the birth of the Christ Child.

He cut down a small pine tree and brought it home. There Luther decorated the tree with lighted candles, which he told his wife and children represented Jesus Christ, the Light of the World. From that small beginning, the popular custom of decorating trees spread throughout Europe and later to America. Early trees were also decorated with small candies and cookies, paper and glass ornaments.

Carefully picked and trimmed with tiny lights — festooned with homemade ornaments and those from friends and travels — our family Christmas tree is more than just a decoration; it's full of memories and shines forth as a symbol of God's love for us.

Tree Trimming Night

*I*n our family we served the same kind of treats each year on tree-trimming night. Our favorites were hot cocoa or cider with cookies. We got out our holiday music tapes and CD's like "The Nutcracker Suite," and "Music Box Christmas," singing along as we decorated the tree and the house.

If your children are grown, invite friends or a young family new to your community to help you decorate the tree. And remember, when you leave your home or are asleep, turn off all lights, including the tree!

Christmas Is For Keeps

It comes every year and will go on forever. And along with
Christmas belong the keepsakes and the customs. Those humble,
everyday things a mother clings to, and ponders, like Mary in the
secret spaces of her heart.

— Marjorie Holmes

Three Ways to Get Your Wings — Be An Angel and...

- Offer to babysit for a single mother so she can go shopping or have time to herself.

- Buy a disposable flash camera and gift certificate for developing for a single parent.

- Give someone a gift that meets a need, and do it anonymously.

Recipe for Christmas Happiness...

Do all the good you can,
By all the means you can,
In all the ways you can,
In all the places you can,
At all the times you can!

— John Wesley

The shepherds had an angel

The wise men had a star;

But what have I,

a little child,

To guide me home from far

Where glad stars

sing together,

And singing angels are?

— Chrstina Rossetti

Each day of the holidays
comes bringing its own gifts.
Open your heart,
Untie the ribbons,
and enjoy the contents!

Scents of Christmas

$\mathcal{A}$ circle of fragrant rosemary and a warm, spicy smell that brings back memories of Christmases past — fill your home with holiday scents for just pennies by making *Homemade Christmas Simmering Potpourri*:

Take the peels of 2 oranges, 3 cinnamon sticks, 12 whole cloves and mix in 2-1/2 cups of hot water. Simmer on the stove on low heat, and your whole house will smell festive and Christmasy.

Victorian Pomander Balls

Take fresh oranges. Stud with whole cloves; use toothpicks to prick holes for the cloves. Then shake in a paper bag filled with powdered cinnamon. Let the pomander balls hang to dry in a warm, airy place for a week or two before tying bright holiday ribbons around them. Give as gifts (wrapped in lace and tied with velvet ribbon), stocking stuffers, or fill a bowl with the fragrant balls to freshen the family room.

Stockings on the Hearth

It is Christmas
in the mansion,
Yule-log fires
and silken frocks;
It is Christmas
in the cottage,
Mother's filling
little socks.

— Anonymous

How to Make a Storytelling Stocking

- First make or purchase a medium to large-size stocking.

- Sew 24 thin ribbons on the outside of the stocking.

- Inside the stocking, place mementos — such as a child's first rattle to a souvenir of a memorable trip or Brownie Scout award.

- Each day, let your child pull one of the items out of the stocking. Tie it to one of the brightly colored ribbons on the outside. As she does, tell the story of its significance.

St. Nicholas and
The First Christmas Stocking

*N*icholas, born in the fourth century in Asia Minor, devoted his life to doing good deeds and became a priest and bishop at a young age. Since his parents had died early, Nicholas was left a fortune, which he spent mainly in giving to the poor and needy.

One day Nicholas heard of the plight of three daughters of an impoverished nobleman. Their mother had died, and in his grief their father made bad business decisions and lost everything, even his castle. Thus he and his daughters had to move to a shabby peasant cottage.

Since he couldn't provide dowries for them or even take care of them, it looked as though they would be sold into slavery.

Hearing of the dire situation, Nicholas rode to their home that night and tossed three bags of gold in the window. They landed in the daughters' stockings, which were hanging by the chimney to dry. With the dowries provided by Nicholas' giving heart, the girls married and lived happily ever after. So the custom evolved of children hanging up their stockings or putting out their shoes in hopes that St. Nicholas would fill them with oranges, candy canes, dolls, wind up cars, chocolates, and other goodies.

The longer one lives

the higher the tower

from which the Christmas bells ring

and the angels sing

and the star of Bethlehem shines,

and so the more splendid is the carillon,

the fuller and sweeter are the heavenly voices,

and the more brilliant is the Light.

— Gladys H. Carroll

Were earth a thousand times as fair

Beset with gold and jewels rare

She yet were far too poor to be

A narrow cradle,

Lord, for Thee.

— Martin Luther

Christmas Isn't Just for Children

The year I turned 34, a friend gave me an Annie doll as an early Christmas gift. I swallowed a hard lump in my throat when I saw her. She represented what my husband, Ken, and I yearned for — a child. We wanted to be more than a couple. We wanted to be a family.

A friend helped me finish stitching a new Victorian Christmas tree skirt. While shopping, I stopped to touch cuddly stuffed animals, and stood mesmerized as a toy train whistled and chugged its way up a hill. *Christmas is for children*, I thought, saddened when I unlocked the door to our too-quiet home.

My thoughts were interrupted by the telephone. "Congratulations," our attorney said. "You have a daughter."

A *daughter*. Time stood still for me. I had to remind myself to breathe. We'd waited so long to adopt. Would it really happen this time? A *daughter*.

Five days before Christmas, our daughter was placed in my empty arms. My daughter, Heather Elise Hemry. At home, I phoned my parents. "You have a new granddaughter!" They shouted for joy. "We'll be there for Christmas," they promised, committing themselves to a seven hour drive.

The days before Christmas slipped by in peaceful preparation. Then, on December 23, an ice storm swept a three-state area. That afternoon, my dad phoned from a hospital in Wichita Falls, Texas.

"We hit ice and slid off the road, down a 90 foot embankment," he said, a tremor in his voice. Wounded but alive, they'd been treated at an emergency room. Their car was wrecked and all roads between us had been closed.

"We've got to get them here," Ken said, calling to rent an airplane. "Since you're a nurse, you go along to take care of them during the flight." A friend came to stay with Heather, and I wept as I kissed her good-bye.

The drive to the airport was treacherous.... It was a white-knuckle flight, but we landed safely in Wichita Falls and picked up my parents. The storm had worsened when we landed at the airport in Oklahoma City. We sent my brother ahead to the terminal while Ken and I helped my parents off the plane in the freezing wind. My brother looked back to see if we needed help, and walked into the wing of the plane. He fell onto the tarmac — unconscious.

By midnight, we were home. Weak and wounded, my family gathered around Heather's crib and wept. On Christmas Eve, my sisters and their families arrived. We piled logs on the fire and locked the door to the blizzard outside. I can't recall a single gift inside those brightly wrapped packages. But etched forever in my memory are the faces gathered there. I'd been given the gift of love and new life. What more could I ask?

— Melanie Hemry

Love and life

That's why He came, and what He offers,

Christmas isn't just for children.

It's for the world.

The little toy dog is covered with dust,
But sturdy and staunch he stands;
And the little toy soldier is red with rust,
And his musket molds in his hands.
Time was when the little toy dog was new,
And the soldier was passing fair,
And that was the time
when our Little Boy Blue
Kissed them and put them there.

— Eugene Field

Little Toy Dolls...Scenes of Christmas Past

Old toy soldiers, dolls, and teddy bears can be used to decorate your tree or house. Pick a spot and arrange a collection of children's worn teddy bears and toys, porcelain dolls in red and white dresses, an old tea set you've found in the attic. Prop the collectibles up on an old trunk and add some wooden alphabet blocks to spell "Merry Christmas" and your scene will bring back memories of Christmases past. Little toys, kids and Christmas have been a delightful combination for decades!

Christmas is Coming

Christmas is coming,
the geese are getting fat,
Please to put a penny in an old
man's hat;
If you haven't got a penny,
ha'penny will do,
If you haven't got a ha'penny,
God bless you.

— Mother Goose

What is Christmas?

Christmas is giving

your last two dollars

to the Salvation Army bellringer

...gladly and cheerfully!

Don't worry if your Christmas card list seems to be growing each year. Instead, be grateful! It just means you're making friends faster than you are losing them.

How to Create a Christmas Newsletter

Writing and sending a family Christmas newsletter is almost like having a little conversation with each friend and family member across the miles. Here's some easy tips for putting yours together this year: Write a one or two page mini-journal chronicling the activities, humor, happenings, and proud, joyful moments of each family member. Ask your spouse and children to help you remember the highlights of the year.

Dress up with computer graphics, rubber stamps, or children's original artwork. Copy on colored paper and scan photographs to add a personal touch!

Friends, in this world of hurry

And work and sudden end

If a thought comes quickly of doing

A kindness to a friend

Do it this very instant!

Don't put it off — don't wait;

What's the use of doing a kindness

If you do it a day too late?

— Unknown

A friend is a present you give yourself.

When they were quite near
they saw that the cottage was made of
gingerbread and covered with cakes,
while the windows were made of
transparent sugar.

— "Hansel and Gretel"

Make a Gingerbread House

*U*se graham crackers and "glue" together the pieces of the Gingerbread House with sugar cement:

Put 3-4 cups of white sugar in a skillet and melt it on high, stirring constantly until it turns brown. Keep the sugar cement hot on the stove while dipping the edges, sides, and roof of the house in the cement before assembling pieces. Press quickly together.

Decorate with tubes of frosting (store-bought or homemade and food-color dyed), marshmallows, gumdrops, M & M's, peppermint, and other candies.

A little child

a shining star

a stable rude,

the door ajar.

Yet in that place

so crude, forlorn,

The Hope of all

the world was born.

— Anonymous

100

Christmas began in the heart of God. It is complete
only when it reaches the heart of man.

— Anonymous

Give a Gift of Memories —
Strengthen the Ties That Bind

*H*ere are some ways to give a priceless gift of family heritage, a legacy of love:

- Gather a family collection of recipes that have been passed down from your grandmother, aunt, mother, and siblings.

- Make a "This is Your Life" album filled with your child's photos from babyhood to the present.

- Make a video tape history of an elderly member of your family, sharing about their first memories, courtship, war experiences, etc.

A Gift of Heritage History

Write a book about your family heritage and involve the whole tribe. Older children and teens can interview grandparents or older family members at Thanksgiving or during a summer reunion using a tape recorder and blank tapes. Then have someone transcribe the oral history into written stories. Add photos and a cover created by the artistic member of the family and send it out as your gift to cousins and extended family.

Christmas Magic is within the human heart, if it is open, in the eyes, if they are lifted up, in the ears, if they are intensely alert; and it is drawn from the Source and the Cause of all wonder which too often seems so far away...but which as Christmas flows so close to us all that if we will but receive it, whoever we are, wherever we are, we are flooded with ecstasy.

— G. H. Carroll

Enjoy the little things this Christmas:

the late-night cup of hot chocolate with your spouse,

the little ornament your child made for you at school,

the sounds of carols sung at church —

for someday we'll turn around, look back,

and realize these were the big,

important things about the season.

We hang everything

on our Christmas tree

Ornaments big and bright

and all of these

sparkling icicles

and twirling balls of white.

— Kay Thompson

"The Rest of the Story..."

Over the years, it's so easy to forget the stories behind favorite ornaments. In a small notebook, write down descriptions of the ornaments, where they came from, who made the ornament, or any special story about them. Store the ornament notebook in the Christmas decorations box so you can supply "the rest of the story" next year.

For the Person Who Has "Everything"

*I*nstead of shopping till you drop for an exotic or unusual gift for the person on your list who has *everything*, purchase something needed by a local agency (such as a warm winter coat for a child who wouldn't otherwise have one). Give the donation in the person's name, and give that person a card with a note about his "gift."

The circle of our Christmas associations and the lessons that they bring, expands! Let us welcome every one of them and summon them to take their place by the Christmas hearth.

— Charles Dickens

Christmas Acrostic Book

*L*et your children make up their own alphabet book of Christmas — a simple acrostic, with the letter and what it stands for and an original illustration on each page. Use white paper, have the child make a cover, and you've created a treasure:

A is for the animals in the stable.

B is for the baby who lay in the hay.

C is for our Christmas tree shining with lights.

D is for dinner with turkey and pumpkin pie.

...and on through the alphabet.

Make a Family Christmas Banner

Sharing a project like designing and putting together a simple Christmas banner to hang in your home is a good way to make a holiday memory.

- Get a large piece of felt or burlap and different-colored squares of felt for symbols and letters, some white glue and scissors.

- Decide together on the symbols you want to portray on your banner: a manger, star, or lamb. You could use a single figure like a dove and the word PEACE, or a star and the words JOY TO THE WORLD.

Display!

What can I give Him,

Poor as I am

If I were a shepherd

I would bring a lamb,

If I were a wise man

I would do my part

Yet what can I give Him?

Give my heart.

— Christina Rossetti

How many observe Christ's birthday!
How few, his precepts!
Oh, it's easier to keep holidays
than commandments.

—Benjamin Franklin

Make a Christmas Basket

A few days before Christmas, create a basket filled with homemade cookies, sliced turkey and special bread, a bright tablecloth and other foods to make a happy meal. Deliver the basket to a family experiencing financial troubles, an elderly person, or a single mother. If she has children, include a few small wrapped gifts to make their Christmas bright.

Reach Out to Those Who Need Fellowship

*I*NVITE a newcomer, an elderly couple, or a friend who will be alone this Christmas to attend your church's Christmas Eve service. Ask ahead of time and include some fellowship time together and snacks shared around the tree before you go.

Cheerfulness is the offset of goodness.

Thanks be to God for His unspeakable Gift —

indescribable
inestimable
incomparable
inexpressible
precious beyond words.

— Lois Lebar

So we will not "spend" Christmas...

nor "observe" Christmas.

We will "keep" Christmas —

keep it as it is...

in all the loveliness

of its ancient traditions.

May we keep it in our hearts,

that we may be kept in its hope.

— Peter Marshall

The Christmas Tissue

*J*ust before Christmas in 1982, my wife, Margaret, and I heard about a family in a nearby town that was experiencing trouble. In fact, their kitchen cupboards were bare. We headed for the grocery store and filled our cart with food for the family.

White Christmases are unusual in Oklahoma, but that night there was a heavy snow covering the ground as we unloaded the groceries. As we chatted with the parents, the four young children were busy inspecting the sacks and putting cereal boxes and fruit away. Suddenly little ten-year-old Charlie bounded from the kitchen with a four-pack of toilet tissue held high in his left hand.

"Look mom, toilet paper!" The mother and father shot a glance at us, with a rather sheepish look on their faces, as Charlie skipped to the bathroom to put away the tissue.

That was a memorable Christmas. I can't remember what gifts we exchanged among the family. Today, years later I have no idea whether I received a tie, new slacks, or what. Nor can I recall what special Christmas musical services we attended. But I'll always remember that scene of Charlie skipping through the house with a pack of toilet tissue held high!

— Dee Stribling

The Gift of Encouragement

When you encourage someone with a positive word, you literally breathe life and hope into his or her life! On your journey through the day, take time to find someone to compliment or affirm: a waiter in a restaurant who graciously serves you, a friend who is thoughtful. Whoever helps you, express how much it means to you. Then watch for the miracles to happen!

> *Where there is love and encouragement, there are always little miracles.*

Give to the world

the best that you have,

And the best

will come back to you.

— Madeline Bridges

Hot Wassail

"Wassail" means "Be in good health," and there's nothing better to warm you up on a chilly night. Here's how to make a pot:

Here we come a-wassailing among the leaves so green. Love and joy come to you, And to your wassail too.

Mix 1 cup sugar, 3 cups water, 4 cinnamon sticks, and 1 T. cloves and allspice with 12 ounces frozen orange juice and lemonade dissolved in 6 cups of water. Stir and bring to a boil. Simmer 1 hour, remove spices, and enjoy!

Christmas Morning Casserole

This recipe is great because it can be made ahead of time and cooked while packages are being unwrapped:

Beat 6 eggs. Add 2 cups milk, 1 teaspoon salt, and 1 teaspoon dry mustard. Gently stir in 1 cup shredded cheddar cheese, 1 pound mild sausage that has been browned and drained, and 4 slices cubed white bread.

Place in a buttered 9" X 13" casserole. Refrigerate overnight. Place in cold oven set at 350 degrees and bake 45 minutes. Serve and watch it disappear!

Villagers all, this frosty tide,

Let your doors swing open wide,

Though wind may follow and snow betide

Yet draw us in by your fire to bide:

Joy shall be yours in the morning.

— Kenneth Grahame

The Origin of the Candy Cane

In the late 1700's in England, all religious symbols, including cross necklaces, were banned from being seen in public. So a candy-maker decided to find a way for Christians to identify each other. He took a piece of white candy to symbolize the purity of the Christ Child. Next he molded the candy in the shape of a shepherd's staff to represent God as the Good Shepherd. Then he wrapped three small red stripes around the candy to signify the Trinity, and a larger red stripe to represent the blood of Jesus Christ, which provides forgiveness of sin.

The Lollipop Tree

*K*ids always ask, "How many days till Christmas?" For the last twelve days, make a "Lollipop Tree," and help them count the days. Cut a white piece of posterboard or heavy cardboard in the shape of a big Christmas tree, and mount it on the child's bedroom door. Decorate the cardboard with a colored tape border and write her name at the top. Buy strips of lollipop for ease in making rows. Put one lollipop at the top of the cardboard for the point of the tree, and then make strips of lollipops in rows. Each day one lollipop gets to be taken off and eaten!

"Christmas is Coming" Paper Chain

*H*elp children count down the days *and* encourage kindness by making a paper chain. Cut red and green construction paper into equal-sized strips, about 1" by 8". On each strip write a simple, enjoyable holiday activity like "Make an ornament today," or "Today take warm mittens to a homeless shelter."

Bring the end of two strips (alternating red and green) together and tape or staple. Continue making links until you have made twenty-five or the days left until Christmas. Each day the child tears off a link and does the activity until all loops are gone and it's Christmas Day!

Here's How to Say "Merry Christmas" in 10 Different Languages:

French:	Joyeux Noel
Spanish:	Feliz Navidad
Danish:	Glaedelig Jul
Finnish:	Houska Joulua
Welsh:	Nadolig Llawen
Swedish:	God Jul
Italian:	Buon Natale
Russian:	S Rozhdestvom Kristovym
German:	Froehliche Weihnachten
Japanese:	Meri Kurisumasu

International Flair

$\mathcal{O}$ne of the best ways to share your customs and learn about Christmas in other countries is to invite an international student from a local university to celebrate the holiday with your family or to spend a weekend in your home during the month of December. The student gets to learn firsthand about American hospitality and traditions and doesn't have to be alone in the dormitory for holidays, as so many international students are. Call a local university or college and ask for the International Student office. You and your family will multiply your joy and make a new friend this season!

If Jesus should tramp the streets tonight
Storm-beaten and hungry for bread,
Seeking a room and a candle light
And a clean, though humble, bed,
Who would welcome the workman in,
Though he came with panting breath,
His hands all bruised and his garments thin —
This workman from Nazareth?

— Edwin Markham

Deck the Halls with Shiny Ribbons

*H*ere are some festive ways to tie up your Christmas with shiny ribbons:

- Tie bright plaid ribbons around lamps and candlesticks.

- Hang a wide red velvet ribbon in a doorway and attach Christmas cards as they arrive.

- Tie bows around throw pillows and a stack of logs by the fireplace.

Edible Cookie Tags

*M*ake cookie tags to adorn gift packages. Use animal or Christmas motif cutters to cut out cookies, and with an ice pick, make a hole in the top of the cookie for stringing thin ribbon through to attach to package. Using different colors of icing to write the names of the recipient. To keep your edible tags fresh, wrap in clear plastic wrap.

The magi, as you know, were wise men — wonderfully wise men who brought gifts to the Babe in the manger. They invented the art of giving Christmas presents.

— O. Henry

Noel, Noel

Angels and shepherds,
Birds of the sky
Come where the Son of God
Doth lie;
Christ on earth with man doth dwell
Join in the shout,
Noel, Noel!

— Bas-Ouercy

A Puzzling Christmas

$\mathcal{T}$he tree is decorated, presents are wrapped (most of them) and stockings are hung from the hearth. What do you do now? Continue the Christmas fun by setting a 1000-piece puzzle out on a table. Invite neighbors, children, grandchildren, and friends over to help complete the puzzle. Hint: snacks will help your puzzle pals stay alert and the puzzle is a great conversation-starter.

If you were busy being kind,
Before you knew it, you would find
You'd soon forget to think 'twas true
That someone was unkind to you.
If you were busy being glad,
And cheering people who are sad,
Although your heart might ache a bit,
You'd soon forget to notice it.

— Rebecca Foresman

Christmas Is Not A Time To Be Mad!

*E*very minute of anger displaces 60 seconds of happiness!

> *For if you forgive men their trespasses, your heavenly Father will also forgive you.*
> Matthew 6:14

Forgiveness is a Christmas gift of the highest value. Write down on a sheet of paper anyone who has hurt you, or any anger you harbor toward another person. Forgive each person on your list, and spend a few minutes praying for them. Then burn the sheet of paper as a sign of your willingness to let go of the anger.

137

When Christmas is Over...

Wrap a small gift in silver or gold for each person to be opened *only* when the tree is dismantled and taken outdoors. Fix snacks and make a party of the un-trimming of the tree. Then to save the environment:

- Take the tree to a recycling program that turns Christmas trees into mulch.

- Take garlands of popcorn to string on outdoor trees for the birds to enjoy.

The Family That Walks
Together ...Stays Trimmer

Start a new tradition this year: The Family Walk. After the Christmas feast has been gobbled, get up from the table and bundle up if necessary. (Everyone! Dishes can be done *after* the walk.) Don't leave anyone behind unless they are ill. Take along the family dog and you'll enjoy walking off a few of the calories just consumed.

Dear Editor:

I am eight years old.

Some of my little friends say there is no Santa Claus. Papa says "If you see it in The Sun it's so." Please tell me the truth; is there a Santa Claus?

Virginia O'Hanlon

Yes, Virginia, There is a Santa Claus.

*H*e exists as certainly as love and generosity and devotion exist, and you know that they abound and give to your life its highest beauty and joy. Alas! how dreary would be the world if there were no Santa Claus! It would be as dreary as if there were no Virginias. There would be no childlike faith then, no poetry, no romance to make tolerable this existence. We should have no enjoyment, except in sense and sight. The eternal light with which childhood fills the world would be extinguished...

— *The New York Sun*, September 21, 1897

Silent Night

*O*n December 24, 1818, in the little village of Oberndorf, Austria, the organ would not work, and the music and carols could not be played for the special Christmas Eve service. Father Joseph Mohr, the parish priest, wrote the words to a new song and asked the organist, Franz Gruber, to compose the tune. That evening "Silent Night," written for two voices and a guitar, was sung in the Christmas Eve service. It became perhaps the most beloved Christmas hymn through Europe and the Americas.

Silent night, holy night!
All is calm, all is bright
Round yon Virgin Mother and Child.
Holy Infant so tender and mild,
Sleep in heavenly peace,
Sleep in heavenly peace.

—Joseph Mohr & Franz Gruber

If we think of our heart,

rather than our purse,

as the reservoir

of our giving,

we shall find it

full all the time!

— David Dunn

Creative Gift Giving

For someone on your gift list, give something of your own that he or she has admired. Attach a card that describes the meaning or the history behind the object you're giving.

> Not what we give
> but what we share —
> for the gift without
> the giver is bare.
> — Jas. Russell Lowell

Christmas Recollections

Sometime soon after Christmas, have a family discussion about your own observance of the holiday. Talk about:

- what you've enjoyed *most*,

- what holiday activity, if discontinued, would make it not seem like Christmas to each of you,

- what one thing you'd like to change about next year's celebration, and

- a new tradition you'd like to try.

The Holly and the Ivy

The holly and the ivy,
When they are both full grown,
Of all the trees that are in the woods,
The holly bears the crown.

The rising of the sun
And the running of the deer,
The playing of the merry organ,
Sweet singing of the choir.

— Old English carol

Are you willing to believe that love is the strongest thing in the world — stronger than hate, stronger than evil, stronger than death — and that the blessed life which began in Bethlehem nineteen hundred years ago is the image and brightness of the Eternal Love? Then you can keep Christmas.

— Henry Van Dyke

Christmas Album and Memory Book

Start a Christmas album so you don't have to wonder each year, "Where's the photo of your first Christmas?" or "Where's that picture of Granddad setting up the train set?"

Here's how: Take a standard or large photo album and cover it in a bright holiday fabric. Insert holiday photos right after Christmas, before they get stuck in a cabinet drawer somewhere. Add photos of kids on Santa's knee, photos of friends and family who visit you during the holidays, and those who send you a holiday photo-cards.

Christmas is for Saying "Thank You"

*M*any people never know if the gifts they sent in the mail were received or enjoyed because writing thank-you notes is almost a lost art among young people! Revive the tradition of writing thank-you notes promptly after Christmas. In your child's stocking, include a box of colorful thank-you notes and stamps so he can express appreciation to grandparents, aunts and uncles, or friends for gifts received at Christmas.

Gratitude is a memory of the heart.

Appreciation is a wonderful thing:
it makes what is excellent in others
belong to us as well.

— Voltaire

And the light shone even brighter.

Will you come and see it?

The light is still there

although the man, his wife and the Child are gone.

I think the light will shine forever.

— Sidney Fields

Happy Birthday, Jesus!

*B*egin a tradition of having a birthday cake for Jesus. Bake a birthday cake on Christmas Eve and decorate it with special care. If you have children, let them help with the mixing and decorating. After Christmas dinner, serve the cake and have everyone sing "Happy Birthday" to Jesus. Since it is a birthday party, bring gifts to the table like canned goods for the hungry in your city, or good toys or clothes that can be donated to needy children.

I will honour Christmas in my heart,
and try to keep it all the year.

— Ebenezer Scrooge

We shall find peace.

We shall hear the angels.

We shall see the sky sparkling

with diamonds.

— Anton Chekhov

The Nativity

J oseph also went up from Galilee, out of the city of Nazareth, into Judea, to the city of David, which is called Bethlehem because he was of the house and lineage of David, to be registered with Mary, his betrothed wife, who was with child. So it was, that while they were there, the days were completed for her to be delivered. And she brought forth her firstborn Son, and wrapped him in swaddling cloths, and laid him in a manger; because there was no room for them in the inn.

— Luke 2:4-7

What a happy New Year for all
if we would carry this same Christmas heart
into every day during the coming year
and make it a permanent thing in our lives.
Let's do it!

— George M. Adams

References

Endnotes

[1]"The Christmas Heart," by George Matthew Adams, *Norman Rockwell's Christmas Book* (Carmel, NY: Guideposts, 1977), p. 116.

[2]"My Christmas Miracle," by Taylor Caldwell, *Norman Rockwell's Christmas Book* (Carmel, NY: Guideposts, 1977), p. 90.

About the Author

Cheri Fuller is a wife, a mother of three grown children, a dynamic speaker, and author of fourteen books. She holds a B. A. in English and History and a Master's Degree in English Literature. Besides being interviewed by hundreds of radio stations in the U.S. and writing aritcles for numerous national magazines, Cheri has served as a consultant and national spokesperson for MCI. She and her family live in Oklahoma City, Oklahoma.

Other books by Cheri Fuller:

Motivating Your Kids From Crayons to Career
Home Life: The Key to Your Child's Success at School
Trading Your Worry for Wonder
Unlocking Your Child's Learning Potential
Home Business Happiness
365 Ways to Build Your Child's Self-Esteem

To contact her, write:
Cheri Fuller
P. O. Box 770493
Oklahoma City, Oklahoma 73177